THE

PR⬤M

BOOK

The Prom Book
The Only Guide You'll Ever Need
by Lauren Metz

First published in 2012 by Zest Books
35 Stillman Street, Suite 121, San Francisco, CA 94107
www.zestbooks.net
Created and produced by Zest Books, San Francisco, CA

Teen Nonfiction / Holidays & Celebrations / Clothing & Dress
Library of Congress Control Number: 2012943321
ISBN: 978-1-936976-28-7

Cover Design: Tanya Napier
Book Design: Marissa Feind, Feind Design
Editor: Daniel Harmon
All photos courtesy of iStock Photo
Typeset in Jensen and Gill Sans

Manufactured in China
SCP 10 9 8 7 6 5 4 3 2 1
4500386849

THE
PRM
BOOK

The Only Guide You'll Ever Need

LAUREN METZ

CONTENTS

Part

PROM PLANNING

Part

PROM DAY

Part

PROM NIGHT

Part

POST PROM

Part

PROM PLANNING

Welcome to your prom! This is such an exciting time, and you've probably been looking forward to it for years! But the road to your magical night can feel bumpy and overwhelming at times. Face it, there's a lot to be done—and that's where this book comes in. I'll walk you through every step, and help you put together your dream prom—from creating a budget to choosing your wheels to finding the perfect look.

How do I know so much about prom and beauty and fashion anyway? Well, I started my career at *Seventeen* magazine, but years before that, I went to three senior proms in just one week. Crazy, right? That was three dates and of course three different dresses, shoes, purses—you name it! I only wish I'd had a book like this back then to help keep me sane and on track!

But I made it out alive, and, more to the point, I also had a great time—three great times, in fact—and so will you! Start your preparations with the Calendar Countdown in Chapter 1, and I'll hold your hand every step of the way from there! Get excited—your big night will be here before you know!

1

YOUR ULTIMATE COUNTDOWN!

Prom's a blast, but let's face it, it also takes a lot of planning. There are appointments to book, countless dresses to try on, and of course there's the issue of finding a date! But don't freak out over your insane to-do list, because—*voila!*—here's your secret weapon for a stress-free prom. This chapter covers everything you'll need to do on a month-by-month basis—so that nothing will slip under the radar and leave you scrambling. Stick to this schedule and prom will be all fun (with no freak outs!).

FEBRUARY: TIME TO GET THE BALL ROLLING!

Prom may feel like it's a long way off, but get the ball rolling now so you're not scrambling later to balance homework, practice, and the search for your dream dress. Three months before your prom—February, in most cases—is the ideal time to start making some decisions.

Get inspired!

Flip through magazines and search online for red carpet looks that catch your eye. Cut or print out your favorites and tape them to your fantasy boards in Chapter 5.

Create a budget

Creating a budget might not be the most exciting part of getting ready for prom (bleh!), but it's a must. Sit down with your parents and use the budget tool on page 20 to get a realistic idea about how much your big night will cost. The good news is that with three months until the big night, there's still plenty of time to save!

Book salon appointments

Hair, makeup, nails, facial ... that's a busy schedule! You don't need to make appointments for all of these—a lot of this stuff you can do your-self!—but call now for the things you want done professionally (that way you'll be able to ensure you get the time slot you really want). Morning appointments are best because you won't panic if the salon is running late. Plus, if you're unhappy with the job they do, you can correct it before your date arrives. Ask about a con-sultation before prom to show your stylist your fantasy board and discuss hair and makeup ideas.

Make a pre-prom plan

If you're going to prom with a group of friends, snapping photos at *everyone's* houses cuts into your

THE DO'S AND DON'TS...
of Prom Planning

DO: Keep the phone number in your cell for every reservation you make until after prom. This makes your life much easier when calling to con-firm—or letting them know you're running late for your appointment.

DON'T: Tweet or post a photo on Facebook of your prom look before the big day—you want your date's jaw to drop when he picks you up!

DO: Enjoy this time. Yeah, there's a lot to do, but planning is part of the excitement and build up. If you start feeling anxious, take a deep breath and just go with the flow. As long as *you* have fun on prom night, that's all that really matters!

precious prep time. Instead, suggest one meeting place where all of your friends and their parents can *ooooh* and *aaaah* together. If you decide on your place, you can surprise everyone with a signature mocktail, photo backdrop, and even a red carpet! Turn to Chapter 11 for more awesome pre-prom party ideas!

Pick your wheels

Set up a lunch date to discuss all transportation details, including a pickup schedule. Do you have enough wiggle room in your budget to splurge on a limo with friends? Then call and request a driver familiar with your neighborhood—a GPS doesn't guarantee he'll make it there on time! Even if rented wheels aren't in your price range, check out Chapter 3 for other swanky options.

MARCH: FINALIZING YOUR LOOK!

You're getting closer! With two months to go, it's about time to locate the dress you really want to wear—because everything from your heels to your bra will depend on the dress you choose.

Find your dream dress!

If you're buying a dress, it's best to shop early so you can call dibs on your style. (Sure, you love your BFF, but both of you wearing red, one-shoulder dresses just won't fly!) Remember to bring your fantasy board as a guide and try on a ton of dresses. You want to find a cut and color that flatter you perfectly. If you're not sure a dress is "the one," don't rush your decision. Instead, ask a salesperson about their policies on refunds and holding gowns, and then visit some other stores.

Go shoe shopping

Your feet naturally swell a bit after walking around all day, so shop later in the afternoon to make sure you're choosing the right fit. You may want flashy stilettos, but they still need to be comfy enough for hours of dancing! Another valuable rule to bear in mind as you look at both shoes and dresses is that long dresses should hit midway down your heel; your dress shouldn't drag on the ground (tripping hazard!), but you don't want your entire shoe to peek out, either.

Choose your bra and underwear

Backless dresses require a special bra and you never want panty lines showing (*ever*). Try on your dress with the underwear you think you'll wear. If anything bunches or feels uncomfortable, the easiest fix is to hit the mall. Bring your dress (or at least pictures of it) so a sales consultant can choose the perfect undergarments for your look. A less expensive alternative for unwanted wiggle room is to remove hooks from a bra you no longer wear and sew those onto the new bra for a customized, tighter fit.

Head to the tailor

Your dress (whether it's brand new or vintage) should fit perfectly, and sometimes that may require a trip to the tailor. Take your shoes, bra, and panties with you to the tailor and request to pick up your dress at least two weeks before prom in case you need a second round of alterations. (Of course, when borrowing a dress, have permission before making any permanent changes.)

Get into a workout routine

Of course your dress is stunning, so now it's time to tone the areas you're flaunting on prom night. Going for a short hemline? Use the calf exercises in Chapter 5 for head-turning legs!

Visit the dermatologist

Clear skin will give you an extra boost of confidence on prom night! Make sure your whole body (face, shoulders, chest, and back!) is pimple-free by starting an acne-clearing regimen now. Some medicated washes and creams may initially irritate your skin or dry it out, so leave enough time for your body to adjust.

Choose to take a date or join a group

Should you ask your crush to prom or go with your girls? Asking that heart-stoppingly adorable guy who you've been crushing on for weeks can be so intimidating! Luckily there are plenty of tips for doing it with confidence later on, in Chapter 6.

APRIL: BRINGING EVERYTHING TOGETHER

Things are really starting to come together. You still have a few calls to make with one month to go—so double-check your appointments, and tie up all those loose ends!

Buy your prom ticket

Holding this in your hand will let it sink in that prom's almost here! (Plus, tickets are often cheaper if you buy in advance.)

Make a reservation

Reservations are essential—especially for large groups. Popular restaurants fill up fast on prom weekends so be the first of your classmates to book a table. If dining out isn't your scene, there are plenty of other options: Pick up pizzas after prom and have a picnic, or plan a potluck dinner with friends.

Decide on an after-prom plan

Don't let your fun fizzle when the last song ends. Throw a slumber party, go midnight bowling, or host after hours at your place.

Confirm all appointments

Make a few quick calls to double-check the time, date, and other information relating to your various appointments. It only takes a few minutes, but gives you plenty of time to make new arrangements if annoying problems pop up.

Accessorize!

Bling! Bling! The right jewelry can work wonders, especially when it comes to more understated looks. Avoid piling too many baubles though—it will take attention away from your dress!

Touch up roots

If you dye your hair noticeably lighter or darker than your natural shade, call now to schedule an appointment one to two weeks before prom. If you color your own hair at home you should *definitely* touch up your color a few weeks before prom. Dye disasters are much more likely at home than at the salon.

If you have a date, order their boutonniere

Call your local florist and ask about discounts for purchasing a matching boutonniere and corsage together. Psst: Don't be shy about letting your date know which colors best match your dress.

ONE WEEK BEFORE: START THE PAMPER PROCESS!

The sooner you can wrap up school assignments and homework, the better! This is going to be a busy week, filled with lots of errands—so be aware: Your time management skills are about to be put to the test.

Give your skin a little extra attention

Breakouts can often happen after a facial, so get yours now—or do it at home for less!

Walk in your shoes

Break in your new heels now so you won't say, "Ouch!" on the big night, or miss out on any fun while you're giving your poor barking dogs a rest. And apply some sandpaper across the bottom of your shoes in advance to give your shoes a little more friction, and help prevent slipping on the dance floor!

Try everything on

Dress rehearsal time! Put on your head-to-toe prom look. If you don't like something, you have one last chance to replace it.

Confirm all appointments one last time

Triple-checking all your prom plans can seem tedious, but it ensures that you won't have any "are you kidding me?!" moments.

THE DAY BEFORE: ADDING THE FINAL TOUCHES!

You've worked extra hard these past few weeks to get ready for prom and now there are only a couple of small things left. Today's more about relaxing and pampering yourself—so take a break and enjoy yourself: You've earned it!

Polish up

Go for a manicure and pedicure with your girlfriends or do your nails together at home. (More on that later!)

Get waxed

Make your skin fuzz-free the day *before* prom. Waxing brows, your upper lip, or arms can leave redness or bumps, so factor in time for any irritation to calm.

Prep your purse

Scrambling to find your camera or instant stain remover on prom day creates stress, so get organized now. Lay out everything that goes in your bag (see the list on page 42) and make sure it fits!

Charge up

Get your tech gear ready to go. Plug in your camera battery (it's not a bad idea to bring an extra one), clear your memory card, and charge your phone so it doesn't fail you during the day tomorrow. Bringing your iPod for the ride to prom? Then charge that, too! BTW, don't freak out if you have photo problems at prom—you can plan a picture swapping party with friends later, or steal the best shots from your friends' Facebook pages.

Get a good night's sleep!

Tomorrow's going to be a very long (and exciting!) day, so hit the sheets early for a solid eight hours of z's.

My Appointments

Appointment: _____

Date and Time: _____

Address: _____

Phone Number: _____

I'm scheduled to see: _____

Notes: _____

_____

_____

_____

Appointment: _____

Date and Time: _____

Address: _____

Phone Number: _____

I'm scheduled to see: _____

Notes: _____

_____

_____

_____

Appointment: _____

Date and Time: _____

Address: _____

Phone Number: _____

I'm scheduled to see: _____

Notes: _____

_____

_____

_____

Appointment: _____

Date and Time: _____

Address: _____

Phone Number: _____

I'm scheduled to see: _____

Notes: _____

_____

_____

_____

Appointment: _____

Date and Time: _____

Address: _____

Phone Number: _____

I'm scheduled to see: _____

Notes: _____

_____

_____

_____

Appointment: _____

Date and Time: _____

Address: _____

Phone Number: _____

I'm scheduled to see: _____

Notes: _____

_____

_____

_____

Appointment: _____

Date and Time: _____

Address: _____

Phone Number: _____

I'm scheduled to see: _____

Notes: _____

_____

_____

_____

Appointment: _____

Date and Time: _____

Address: _____

Phone Number: _____

I'm scheduled to see: _____

Notes: _____

_____

_____

_____

2

BREAKING DOWN THE BUDGET

Prom's just one night, but it requires a budget-balancing act that begins months in advance. You'll need to keep asking yourself: "Where can I save, and what's worth the splurge?" Sure, there will be a ton of things to keep track of—limo! dress! dinner!—but this guide is here to help you stay on top of everything. Prom doesn't need to be wildly expensive, and this chapter will help you smartly plan (and shop!) so you only spend as much or as little as you want.

SETTING A BUDGET

How much can you afford to spend? Add up the amounts below to get your magic number.

My parents are willing to contribute $ _____

I have already saved $ _____

Before prom I can expect to earn and save $ _____

TOTAL   **$** _____

MAKING YOUR BUDGET WORK FOR YOU

Every time you make a purchase (or find another cheaper way to check something off the lists below), write the exact amount you spent and then update your total at the bottom. When you record everything you buy, you'll know exactly how much moolah you have left in your budget, and your spending won't ever spiral out of control. (Plus, you won't overlook any key items that you're going to need on prom night, like the right bra and panties.)

CHECKLIST 1: The Look	HOW MUCH I SPENT
Dress	$ _____
Shoes	$ _____
Purse	$ _____
Jewelry	$ _____
Underwear	$ _____
Alterations	$ _____
Other	$ _____
TOTAL	**$** _____

CHECKLIST 2: Beauty	HOW MUCH I SPENT
Consultation appointment	$ _____
Hair appointment + tip	$ _____
New hair accessories	$ _____
Makeup appointment + tip	$ _____
New makeup products	$ _____
Facial	$ _____
Manicure and pedicure	$ _____
Spray tan	$ _____
Roots touch up	$ _____
Waxing	$ _____
Other	$ _____
TOTAL	$ _____

 When making your hair and makeup appointments, ask if your stylist will include a free consultation.

CHECKLIST 3: Wheels, Meals ect.	HOW MUCH I SPENT
Transportation	$ _____
Your date's boutonniere	$ _____
Prom ticket	$ _____
Dinner	$ _____
Professional photos	$ _____
After-prom plans	$ _____
Other	$ _____
TOTAL	**$** _____

 TIP Stage your own photo shoot with your BFFs. Learn how in Chapter 12.

MY TOTAL SO FAR $ _____

(Use pencil to write this number so you can erase and update.)

FIVE FUN WAYS TO EARN MONEY FOR PROM!

Need a way to earn cash that works with your schedule? Try out one of these ideas, and watch your bank account fatten up.

Clean out your garage

Do your parents a favor and offer to go through those old boxes collecting dust in the garage and attic. Take the things they no longer want and sell them on eBay.

Run errands

Have your license? Ask your parents and family members to spread the word that you're available to pick up groceries or dry cleaning or do any other driving-oriented chores for an hourly rate.

> ### REAL TALK
> *"When asking your parents to help pay for prom, you need to clearly explain to them how much everything will cost. Show them your list of purchases—they may not be aware of all the little things that can add up. Asking to split the bill is fair. If they don't agree to that, then discuss borrowing money and ways you can reimburse them over the summer."*
>
> —Marcus Dixon, age 18
> San Francisco, California

Sign up for email alerts from discount sites like Bloomspot, Groupon, and Living Social. You'll find deals in your area for manicures, facials, waxing, and more! Just check that the expiration date isn't *before* prom.

Become a tutor or coach

Already babysit? Charge more and include private lessons in a subject that you especially excel at, or offer one-on-one training in the sport that you love.

Assist with party planning

Busy parents can always use a second set of hands when planning their kids' birthday parties. Offer to showcase your creativity and make one-of-a-kind invitations or bake dozens of cupcakes. Around the holidays, you can also be a kitchen helper for family friends throwing big parties.

Show off your photography skills

Besides baking and passing around hors d'oeuvres, you can also snap candid pics or videos at parties. The hosts are often too busy greeting guests and mingling to capture those special moments, so that's where you can readily step in. After the night, put images on a disc and stand out by buying an inexpensive frame for the best photo. When you give both of those to whomever hired you, you can count on them recommending you to their friends!

THE DO'S AND DON'TS...
of Money Matters

DO: Clean out your closet. Place clothing you no longer wear but is still in good condition on eBay along with your parents' stuff.

DO: Be extra cautious when looking for odd jobs online. You can find posts to run errands on Craigslist, but always put your safety before a paycheck. Working for family or friends of family members is your best option.

DON'T: Stop earning money after prom. If you have a booming babysitting business don't put it on hold after prom! Keep up the good work and save some money for college or a car.

LEARNING TO EARN

Money has the potential to cause real conflict. Luckily, you can keep things tidy and keep your stress levels low by sticking to your budget—and those hire-me! ideas could even earn you more money than you actually spend on prom. Profit!

> ### REAL TALK
> *"I got my makeup done at a department store so it was free (although you're usually expected to purchase one or two of the products used on your look)."*
> —Emma Glickman, age 16
> Livingston, New Jersey

Borrow! Borrow! Borrow! After you decide on a dress, ask your mom, friends, or aunts if you can take a peek at their jewelry boxes for matching accessories. If you don't already own the perfect purse and shoes for your look, ask to borrow those for the night, too! When you return the pieces, be sure to write a thank you note or buy the lender a small gift to show your appreciation.

WHO PAYS: YOU OR YOUR DATE?

You buy the boutonniere and he gets the corsage, but what about everything else?

REAL TALK

He Says:

"If a guy asks a girl to prom, unless he is not in the financial position to do so, he should pay for everything— except transportation, which should be split. Since the boy asked the girl, he should make it a worry-free and enjoyable experience for her. Prom is like an amazing (and expensive!) date. However, if the girl asks the guy, then they should split all of the costs. It's common courtesy for the guy to pay and splitting is a fair compromise."

—Eric Lederman, age 15
Martinsville, New Jersey

She Says:

"Your date should pay for transportation and dinner, but you should split the cost of prom tickets and post-prom activities. Your date should not have to pay for everything— prom is expensive!"

—Alexandra Sincan, age 17
Sherman Oaks, California

3

BOOKING YOUR WHEELS

How will you make your grand entrance at prom? There are a lot of options to consider—everything from hiring a limo to renting a party bus to getting an older brother to drive you for free. Whichever mode of transportation you choose, it's important to remember that it's only one part of a pretty long night—so before you sign on any dotted line (or monopolize your sibling's Saturday night), make sure that it fits into your budget and will get you everywhere you need to go. Check out the options below, and figure out what works best for you!

QUICK TIP!

Steer clear of taking public transportation late at night for safety reasons, and don't rely on calling a cab. On a busy Friday or Saturday night, cabs could take over an hour to arrive and you can't hold them responsible if they don't show at all. But no matter how you're getting to prom, cover your bases by preparing a backup plan. Have someone on speed dial who can pitch in if your limo gets a flat, if the friend who planned to take you suddenly feels sick, or if any other driving disaster strikes.

HIRING A LIMO

While booking a limo is a traditional approach, going that route can take a major chunk out of your budget. If you want to splurge on a limo and save in other places, then go for it! But if you'd rather splurge on hair and makeup or buy a more expensive dress, you'll still arrive to prom in style—promise! Consider the pros and cons . . .

PROS:

► When you and your BFFs bounce from dinner to prom to the after party all together, there's no missing out on a single moment of fun!

► Are you still getting to know your date? If so, riding alone with him could feel sort of awkward—and put stress on you to keep the conversation going. Being in a group takes the pressure off, so you can relax and have a good time.

► C'mon—unless you were the magazine-selling champion at your middle school, how often do you get the chance to go cruising around in a limo?

CONS:

► Hiring a chauffeur for the night doesn't come cheap! Unless you're lucky enough to have an unlimited budget, renting a limo means you'll have to give up something else.

► When you're depending on someone to take you where you need to be, there's a long list of things that could potentially go wrong: The driver could get lost or not show up at all, or you might get a different vehicle from the one you thought you ordered, or you could run into "hidden fees," or ... well you get the picture now, right?

► This is the biggest one: Renting a limo with a group means mixing friends and money, which can get tricky. If someone doesn't pay their share on time—or if (reality check!) someone gets sick in the limo and a parent's credit card is billed for the cleanup—your friendship could feel the strain.

Things you need to know

Take your time making a decision about transportation, and ask your parents for their input. If you and your friends agree that you want a limo to be part of your prom experience, lock down exactly who will be in your group and then get rental savvy before signing a contract.

Step 1: Do your research. Ask older classmates and friends for their recommendations. When searching online for local limo companies, read the reviews. Choose a company whose reputation you feel completely confident in.

Step 2: Make multiple calls. Compare prices with a few reputable companies—but don't tell them you're interested in renting a limo for prom. Why? Your big night puts blinged-out dollar signs in their eyes! If one company gives you a lower price, ask the others to match or beat it. Here are the important questions you'll need to ask:

YOUR OPTIONS: Choose a limo style that fits your needs—and personality!

VINTAGE CAR
When you really want to stand out, choose a rental no one else will have!

Seats: 2
Price: From $75/hr per person

STRETCH SUV LIMO
Go ahead—feel like a celebrity for the night!

Seats: 15-20
Price: From $10/hr per person

➤ *Do you require a minimum number of hours?* Most places will say three or four.

➤ *What are the additional fees?* Companies can charge extra for tolls, gas, cleaning before and after, cancellation fees, and more. Forcing them to be upfront protects you from expensive surprises later.

➤ *Is gratuity included?* Expect to give a good driver a 15 to 20 percent tip for the night.

➤ *What are your rental options for a group my size?* Planning on splitting the cost with a lot of people? That will save you money, but some companies may have a limit on how many people can ride together. Get confirmation that they can accommodate everyone comfortably—no squeezing twelve people into a ten-seater.

STRETCH LIMO
Kick off the fun with a group of your closest friends. If there's an iPod or iPhone connection in the limo, create a special prom playlist for the ride.
Seats: 6-12
Price: From $15/hr per person

PARTY BUS
It's more difficult to organize a group this large, but having everyone together will be a party of its own.
Seats: 20
Price: From $10/hr per person

TROLLEY LIMO
Put a unique spin on the party bus!
Seats: 20
Price: From $10/hr per person

Step 3: Get it in writing.
Make sure you cover every last detail in your contract: that includes the price, all possible fees, pick-up and drop-off times and locations, and the limo style and color. Preferably, sign the contract at their office instead of emailing or faxing it. That way, you can see the exact model you're renting and take pictures. If you notice something missing in the contract, write it down, initial and date it, and ask the manager to do the same before making anything official. Keep a signed copy of the contract (with all changes included and approved) for your records.

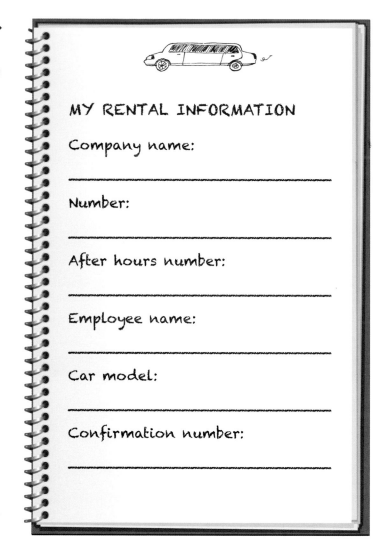

MY RENTAL INFORMATION

Company name:

_____

Number:

_____

After hours number:

_____

Employee name:

_____

Car model:

_____

Confirmation number:

_____

Step 4: Confirm, confirm, confirm! Call your rental company one month before prom to make sure they have all the details correct. Then call again the week before prom to confirm everything once more, and also send detailed directions for the night—your driver shouldn't rely only on GPS!

WHAT ARE MY OTHER TRANSPORTATION OPTIONS?

Rent a town car

You most likely won't have the privacy window between you and the driver like you would in a limo, but this choice still has a luxe vibe. Even better? Two couples can split the cost if someone agrees to ride shotgun.

Have a friend drive

If asking a parent to play driver for the night is a social disaster, then turn to an older sibling or friend. Offer to pay to have their car cleaned for prom (you don't want to sit on fast-food crumbs!), and remember to do something nice to thank them.

Drive yourself!

There's no worrying about a late driver when you take your own wheels!

4

WHAT ABOUT DINNER?

Some schools plan for a nice dinner to be served at prom, although those tickets are usually expensive. Whether you plan on having dinner next to the dance floor or making a reservation at your town's fanciest restaurant, here are a few universal rules to chew on.

DINNER DO'S

Do: *Place a napkin on your lap.* Sure, it's an old rule of etiquette, but that napkin can also catch a ketchup catastrophe before it splatters on your dress. Eek!

Do: *Have an instant stain remover handy.* Spills happen, so arm yourself with a stick or wipes that will magically erase any whoops moments.

Do: *Keep floss and mints in your purse.* Once you finish eating, head to the bathroom for an is-there-food-in-my-teeth? check. Freshen up your breath now because you never know what can happen while slow dancing later.

DINNER DON'TS

Don't: *Order spaghetti.* Or a dish with garlic. Or anything with a sauce that could cause a dress disaster. Instead, opt for a light meal that can be cut into small pieces, like grilled chicken or fish; a heavy dish won't feel so comfortable when you're busting moves on the dance floor.

Don't: *Get adventurous with the menu.* If you've never tried something before, now is not the time to expand your palate. How come? Besides not liking your meal, there's always the possibility that an allergic reaction or an upset stomach could put a serious damper on your night!

Don't: *Feel self-conscious about eating in front of your date.* You'll need energy to make it through the night, so dig in! You should enjoy it! And as long as you chew with your mouth closed and avoid telling stories while salmon's swooshing around your mouth, you're good to go.

EATING AT A RESTAURANT

Going out to eat with a group? Make the reservation at least one month in advance (remember, popular places fill up fast!) and ask the restaurant if they have a private room available for your party that doesn't come at an additional cost. Dining out with a big group can get tricky—especially when the check comes—so you'll want answers to the following questions before you tell the hostess you've arrived.

The Menu: You should definitely inquire in advance about the restaurant's prix fixe options, which offer several courses for the same price (and make splitting the bill easier!). If everyone in your group orders different meals, but you still plan to split the bill evenly, don't be that person who orders the most expensive thing on the menu!

Paying the Bill: Ask ahead of time if everyone in your party will be able to pay using their own credit or debit cards. (Some places may say no-way to charging fourteen cards!) Telling everyone in advance to bring cash may be your easiest option. If that's the case, your group should have a mix of bills so dispersing change won't turn into an SAT-worthy math problem.

How Much Should You Tip? You should generally tip between 15 to 20 percent of the total bill. When eating with a large group, use the calculator on your phone (or the algebra whiz at your table) to find out how much 18 percent is. Divide that by the number of people in your party and round up to the nearest dollar. That's how much everyone should add to their share.

Less Formal Dining Options

Potluck Prom Party: Have your friends (or their parents) drop off a plate of their favorite food to your house in the afternoon. Then you can all feast together buffet-style before or after prom. Use the drink recipes in Chapter 14 to add the wow factor to your dinner party.

Pizza Picnic: Before prom, pack a large blanket and scout out the perfect picnic location. Then take your limo to the local pizza place and order your favorite pies. Ask for plenty of napkins and cups, and pick up a few cold drinks. Eating under the stars has never been more fun!

Diner: Skip the fancy-schmancy restaurant scene and opt for a dessert party at a nearby diner. Order an assortment of pies, puddings, cakes, and shakes to share. Hello, chocolate heaven!

THREE WAYS TO EAT OUT FOR LESS

1 Skip the appetizers—or at least split them between two or three people. For something free to munch on before your dinner arrives, ask your server for complimentary bread and olive oil. Sprinkle a little salt and pepper into the olive oil and you have a tasty dip that cost zero bucks.

2 Choose a restaurant that you know has large portions. Splitting an entrée with your date or BFF will substantially cut down your tab.

3 Stick to water. Sodas and other sweetened drinks can wind up adding a lot to your tab. You'll need to be hydrated for all that dancing later on, but there's no need to go beyond water here. And if you really want something sweeter (or more caffeinated) later on, there's a vending machine at most venues.

5

PLANNING YOUR LOOK

There's nothing better than getting all dressed up and dancing the night away with your friends. But the sad truth is that there's not a lot of nights like this, so you have to make it count. The fashion flow chart included below will help you pick a style that allows your personality to really shine. Let's get started so you can get shopping!

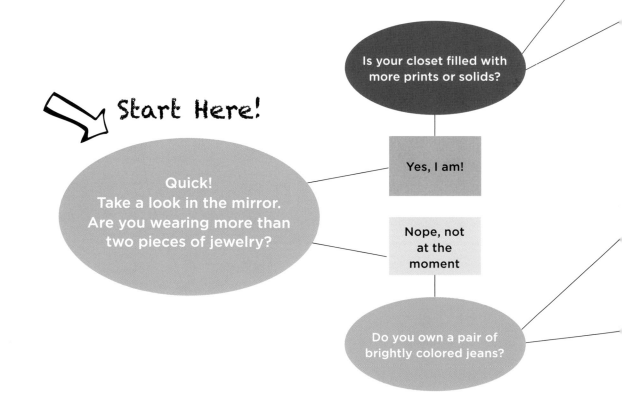

Start Here!

Quick!
Take a look in the mirror.
Are you wearing more than
two pieces of jewelry?

Is your closet filled with
more prints or solids?

Yes, I am!

Nope, not
at the
moment

Do you own a pair of
brightly colored jeans?

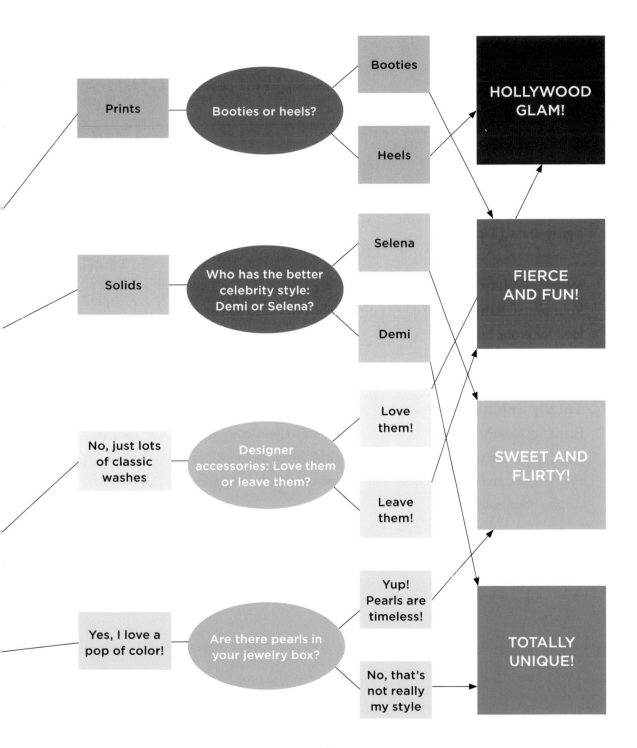

Hollywood glam!

Bring on the sparkle! A dress that flaunts your silhouette adds to the fashion drama, so keep jewelry to a minimum. The real showstopper will be your glitzy gown, so your baubles and makeup should flatter it—not compete.

Fierce & fun!

Some girls may be too intimidated to take fashion risks at prom, but not you. Your urban-chic style gives off a badass vibe, so choose edgy accessories that toughen up a girly dress! (Tip: Use a wild cocktail ring to instantly punch up your look.)

Sweet & flirty!

Your overall fashion vibe is chic-meets-sophisticated. Keep your trademark polished look for prom, but add an unexpected twist to take the night to the next level. Try a sexy, one-shoulder cut, or a dress with hints of peekaboo lace.

Totally unique!

Blending into the crowd isn't your thing (at all!). Everything you throw on pops with personality and your prom dress shouldn't be an exception. Check out vintage shops, thrift stores, and sites like Etsy.com for one-of-a-kind accessories and purses that display your individuality.

ACCESSORIZE YOUR LOOK!

Choose the right purse and jewelry for head-to-toe prom night perfection!

Purses

When you think about accessories you need to buy or borrow for prom, a purse might not be the first thing that pops into your mind. But a purse is important; aside from the fact that it provides the perfect place to stash your stuff, the right bag can also subtly enhance your entire look.

Sparkle: Take glam to the next level with a glittery purse. It's like an extra piece of jewelry!

Fringe: Throw an unexpected punch into your look with this boho-fabulous trend.

Quilted: Channel your inner Audrey Hepburn with a sophisticated pattern.

Bright: A strong pop of color electrifies your look!

Studded: Use edgy pieces for a haute couture rocker vibe. Chains are another fun option!

Animal print: It's fierce without trying too hard.

What to Carry in Your Purse

Prom tickets (and school ID if it's required)

Camera (and an extra battery), if you don't have a camera phone

Money (for limo driver, dinner, keepsakes, and after prom plans)

Directions for your limo driver

Cell phone

House keys

Breath mints or gum

Floss

Lip-gloss

Foundation or concealer for touch-ups

Tissues

Tampons

Three safety pins (for a dress emergency!)

Cuticle scissors

Instant stain remover

Aspirin

Mini mirror

Travel-size deodorant

Cotton swabs (to clean up runny makeup)

Jewelry

Flashy pieces let you put your own spin on a prom dress, so even if—gasp!—another girl walks in wearing the same dress, your look will still be unique. You don't need to purchase all new jewelry for prom either. Instead, you can mix and match with borrowed pieces, and use costume jewelry for a major splash that costs next to nothing.

Statement necklace: Inject glam into your look with a bold piece of jewelry, but let it make a real impact by complementing it with a simple dress and minimalist earrings.

Vintage bangles: Scour thrift stores for one-of-a-kind accessories and layer these bracelets to fit your taste.

Cocktail ring: Need an instant touch of luxe? Just slip this on!

Pearls: These baubles are timeless, but experiment with colored pearls to add some energy.

Chandelier earrings: Wear your hair up so you can really show these off! Bonus: Because they're just the right amount of over-the-top, you don't need to spend extra money on a necklace!

Layered necklaces: Mix and match with different lengths and styles to breathe excitement into a solid dress.

RAMONA BRAGANZA'S PERFECT PROM WORKOUT

Once you know what kind of dress you're going to wear and how you're going to wear it, it's time to focus on the features you plan to really show off—and celebrity trainer Ramona Braganza is on hand to help!

Ramona's one of the top personal trainers in the world. She's worked with Jessica Alba for the past 12 years, and her other Hollywood clients include A-listers like Halle Berry, Anne Hathaway, Jessica Biel, Kate Beckinsale, Amanda Seyfried, Eva Mendez, and Scarlett Johansson— and now she's right here to help you get fit for prom! Depending on the style of your dress, you can follow Ramona's specialized 3-2-1 Training Method four times each week. You'll get toned and lean in just four to six weeks!

HOW IT WORKS

Ramona's celebrity clients follow a "3 Cardio, 2 Circuit, and 1 Core" training routine. Below are the "Circuit" workouts, which each consist of three moves that are done consecutively. So select the circuit that's the best match for your dress, and get down to business!

CIRCUIT ONE: SCULPT YOUR BICEPS FOR STRAPLESS OR ONE-SHOULDER DRESSES

Touch the sky: Standing tall, hold three-pound dumbbells (or one-liter water bottles) in each hand. Bend elbows and bring dumbbells to ear level with palms facing forward. Straighten arm and press one dumbbell at a time up toward the ceiling, alternating arms. Do each side 20 times.

Push–ups: Begin in a standard pushup position, placing your hands slightly closer than shoulder width apart. Keeping elbows tucked into your sides, bend arms and slowly lower your body to slightly above the ground. Push yourself back up and keep your body in a straight line. Repeat 12 times.

Twisting punches: Stand with your feet hip-width apart, knees slightly bent, and hold a three-pound weight in each hand. Twist your body to the left and punch your right arm straight out and across your body to the left. Then twist your body to the right, return right arm with elbow bent at the side, and simultaneously punch left arm. Repeat continuously, twisting and punching with abs contracted for a total of 20 times.

CIRCUIT TWO: GET SEXY LEGS FOR SHORT DRESSES

Squats: Begin by holding three- to five-pound dumbbells in each hand and stand with your feet slightly wider than shoulder-width apart. Lower yourself until your thighs are parallel to the ground and lean back to the point where you can almost reach your toes. Hold for three seconds then rise up by squeezing your glutes and pushing your hips forward to stand tall. Repeat 20 times.

Forward alternating lunges: Begin by holding three- to five-pound dumbbells in each hand with your arms by your sides and feet together. Take a giant step forward with your right leg landing gently with a bent knee (Don't let your right knee move past your toes). Pause in a ninety-degree bend, then push off your right foot back to return to the beginning position. Alternate with the left leg for a total of 20 times.

Diagonal reverse lunge punches: Begin by standing tall with feet together and arms by your sides. Take a giant step back with your right leg as you simultaneously stretch your left arm diagonally to the ceiling and touch the ground with your right hand. Return to start, then repeat the same side for 10 times total. Repeat with the left leg raising right arm up 10 times total.

CIRCUIT THREE: WORK YOUR GLUTES AND ABS FOR BODY-HUGGING DRESSES

Squat jumps: Begin by standing with your feet together, then squat down and place your hands on the ground. Next, kick your feet out as if you're doing a pushup, with your body making a straight line. Pause for a moment, kick your feet back in toward your tummy, and jump up while keeping your knees slightly bent. Repeat 10 times.

Bench sit-ups: Begin by standing in front of a bench, facing away. Bend your knees, keeping your abs contracted. Without using your hands, sit on the bench and lower your body back to the lying position. Contract your abs and roll up to a sitting position, then push on your heels to stand. Repeat 10 times.

Leg lifts: Lie on your back and place your hands under your butt. Inhale, and while exhaling lift your legs ninety degrees with knees slightly bent. Inhale, and slowly lower, them stopping about six inches above the ground. Raise legs back up and then lower again, keeping your lower back touching the floor and your neck in neutral position. Repeat for 10 times.

PUTTING IT ALL TOGETHER

Now it's time to turn your selected Circuit moves into the complete 3-2-1 workout. Here's the order to do your 3 Cardio, 2 Circuit, and 1 Core exercises.

CARDIO 1: Dance for one song.

CIRCUIT 1: Do your three Circuit moves from the previous pages. Take a thirty-second water break and then do them again.

CARDIO 2: Go up and down your stairs for one song. (You can also step up and down on a low bench.)

CIRCUIT 2: Do your three Circuit moves above. Take a thirty second water break and then do them again.

CARDIO 3: Jump rope for one song. (You can also dance or jog around, too.)

CORE: Finish your workout with a Core exercise called "plank" (see page 44).

> **Step 1:** Begin by lying on your stomach and propping yourself up on your forearms with palms down.

> **Step 2:** Inhale, dig toes into floor, and raise up into plank position by forming a straight line from your shoulders to your heels, keeping head down.

> **Step 3:** Keep belly button pulled into spine and breathe without letting your back sway. Hold this position for thirty seconds, and work your way up to a minute.

If you're an exercise beginner, don't push yourself too far out of your comfort zone at the start. Set your own pace and each time add a few more moves to your specialized 3-2-1 routine. And don't give up working out once prom is over. Take the cardio moves outside in the summer and bike around the block or jump rope in your yard.

Your Fantasy Board — Dresses

You can use these pages to showcase the dresses that you love from your favorite print and online sources.

Your Fantasy Board — Accessories

You can use these pages to showcase the jewelry, purses, and shoes that you love from your favorite print and online sources.

Your Fantasy Board — Hair

You can use these pages to showcase the hair that you love from your favorite print and online sources.

6

NAVIGATING THE DATING SITUATION

Prom's all about glamming up and having the most fun possible—so you definitely want to spend the night with people who are on the same page as you. If you already have a boyfriend, it's probably a given that you're going together. (Although, if your relationship has been rocky lately, seriously consider making it a girls' night instead to prevent a tears-in-the-bathroom situation.)

Now for all the single ladies, you can either ask that oh-so-hot guy you've been crushing on or go with your buds, whether in a big group or as a couple with your best guy friend. But how do you know if you should take the risk and ask your crush to be your arm candy for the night? Take this quiz to find out!

DUE FOR A DATE?

Use this checklist to figure out whether your crush deserves to be upgraded to prom date.

TRUE

You think a lot of guys are cute, but there's only one who you daydream about. ☐

Every now and then, you catch your crush staring at you (in a cute way—not creepy!). ☐

It's more than just textual: You also talk to him on the phone. ☐

Your crush is 100 percent single—no potential ex drama for you! ☐

He already knows your friends and gets along great with them. ☐

You know his friends—and like them, too. ☐

He's invited you somewhere in the past month. ☐

He's already hinted to you about going to prom. ☐

Your crush isn't all over you and super touchy-feely when you're alone. (Read: He's not going to expect sex!) ☐

He ignores his phone when you're together. ☐

You're always in a good mood after spending time with him. ☐

He asks you questions to get to know you better. ☐

Now, count how many times you checked off TRUE.

Less than six?

Go with friends! Your crush may be into you, but he's not really demonstrating the necessary evidence that he'd make an awesome prom date. When you decide to go with friends, you don't have to worry about anyone bailing at the last minute, or stress about awkward moments and unnecessary pressure. Going with friends ensures you'll have an *ahhh-mazing* time, because these are already the people who make you laugh and smile the most!

Six or more?

Go for it! This guy already makes you feel relaxed and happy, so you'll be able to let your guard down at prom and have a great time. You can hope that he'll make it easy and ask you first, but don't wait too long. After all, he could be shy, or afraid you'll say no—and in the meantime someone else could always ask him out! If he hasn't asked you to prom with a month to go, it's time to make your move. Here's how:

When to ask him: Wait until you're alone—you don't want the pressure of a large group weighing down on you. Texting seems less sincere, so it's better to ask him in person. You don't want to overthink this part. (It will only make you more nervous!) It can be as easy as waiting for him by his locker after school.

What to say: Bring up prom in a casual way, like saying you can't believe it's only a month away. Then throw in a flirty and witty line, like, "So, since Channing Tatum still hasn't replied to my text about prom, would you want to go with me instead?" and smile! That shows you're relaxed even though it's a jittery situation.

If he says yes: Congrats! Tell him you can't wait to see his moves on the dance floor, but don't worry about figuring out all the details now. You can give him a call closer to prom to talk about who's buying the tickets and paying for dinner, where he'll need to meet you before prom, what color flowers best match your dress, and more.

In case he says no: Hearing that may leave a pit in your stomach or make you feel silly for asking him, but don't. It took a lot of guts to put yourself out there, so be proud. Show off your easy-going confidence by letting him know that you understand and by not making it a big deal. You can even make a joke, like, "Well, I guess I'll have to hold my own purse all night now." Leave the conversation quickly and on a sweet note by saying something along the lines of, "I have to go meet my friends for lunch, but I'll see you later." And smile! That lets him know you're still going to have an awesome time.

Notes

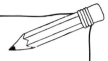

Notes

Notes

Part

PROM DAY

Hey there, gorgeous! You won't need a fairy god-mother to transform into a breathtaking beauty on prom night, because this section is bursting at the seams with valuable A-list knowledge! For starters, celebrity dermatologist Dr. Murad tells you how to get glowing skin in time for prom, while former *Seventeen* magazine beauty editor Meredith Gray shares makeup tips (like teaching you to apply faux lashes and choosing the right blush for your skin tone) that you'll be able to use forever!

Hold on, there's more! Pam Kelly, the whiz behind Fantastic Sams hair salons, gives you directions for six head-turning hairstyles, and celebrity eyebrow guru Elke von Freudenberg gets your face red carpet ready!

Whew! After you've figured out how to look your very best, you can turn your focus to throwing the perfect pre-prom bash! Learn how to create your own photo opportunity in Chapter 12 (and psst: there's even advice to help you take the perfect photo every time). After all that, the only question left is, "Are you ready to party?"

7

YOUR PROM DAY SCHEDULE

It's. Finally. Here! For months you've been eagerly counting down the days until you could treat yourself to a head-to-toe beauty glamformation, put on your perfect dress, and dance the night away with your friends. You're in the home stretch now, so keep the final hours running smoothly with this countdown. You'll power up in the morning, stay organized throughout the day, and even squeeze in some time to relax. Now let's get your big day started!

MORNING:

9:00: Good morning, sunshine! Start your day with a power breakfast—you're going to need your energy! Whip up an omelet and load it with fresh veggies, or sip on celebrity trainer Bobby Strom's power blend (included in the sidebaron the next page).

9:30: Take a relaxing bath, and shave now. Moisturize with a shimmering lotion to give your skin a subtle glisten.

10:30: Swing by the florist and pick up your date's boutonniere.

11:00: Beauty time! Head to your hair and makeup appointments with your fantasy boards in hand. Wear a button-down shirt so you won't have to pull your top over your head to get it off—that could really mess up your hairstyle! If a parent or a friend is

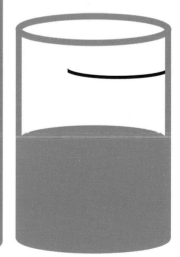

Start Your Day Right!

If you have a juicer at home, celebrity trainer Bobby Strom—he's worked with Jennifer Lopez, Scarlett Johansson, and Blake Lively!—is on hand to offer you his recipe for a drink guaranteed to keep you energized while on the go today. The many green ingredients may not scream "yum!" but Bobby promises the taste will surprise you (in a good way!). "This is what Blake Lively had everyday on the set of *How fitting*.

Ingredients:
1/2 bunch of kale
Handful of spinach
2 pieces of romaine lettuce
Small bunch of parsley
1/2 cucumber
1 stalk celery
1/2 green apple
1/3 of a lemon
(Note: Leave skins on for the most nutrients!)

waiting with you, ask them to snap candid shots that you can add to your scrapbook in the back of this book.

AFTERNOON:

1:00: Time for lunch! Eat a meal that won't leave you feeling bloated when it's time to zip up your dress later. Go for a veggie or turkey wrap, or a salad topped with tuna or chicken and a light dressing.

1:30: Do something relaxing now, like read a book or watch TV.

3:00: Get your purse ready for tonight (see page 42 for everything you need to bring) and set out your jewelry, shoes, and dress. Rip off any tags so you can just slip right into your look. If you're doing your own hair and makeup, flip to Chapters 9 and 10 for advice from the pros and get started.

4:30: Eat a light snack, like celery and peanut butter, or wholegrain crackers and low-fat cheese.

5:00: Do any last minute hair and makeup touch ups. It's almost time for your grand entrance!

> ### THE DAY BEFORE
> New York City nutritionist and a member of *Cosmopolitan's* Health Advisory Board Stephanie Middleberg suggests you skip the after-dinner snack the night before prom. But if you must, choose one that's less than 150 calories so you'll still feel energized the next morning —no food hangover! Also, sip on warm water with lemon before bed. Lemon serves as a natural diuretic, meaning this pre-dreams drink will aid in digestion and reduce water retention so you wake up feeling lean.

6:00: Get dressed for prom! Turn on music to pump yourself up.

AVOID THAT BLOATED FEELING ON PROM DAY

Some foods will slow you down and leave your skin dull, so you end up looking and feeling blah. Don't let that happen on prom day with Stephanie's menu of must-do's:

Good: High Potassium Foods

Bananas, coconut water, and avocados all off-set sodium, which causes your body to feel puffy.

Good: Debloating Veggies

Like warm water with lemon, asparagus and cucumbers help with breaking down food and flushing out water.

Bad: Sauces

Many sauces are very high in sugar and salt, which can make you feel uncomfortable. When looking at a label, % DV (daily value) should be under 20% per serving.

Bad: Diet Foods

Step away from the low-fat cookies and diet soda. Foods that contain artificial sweeteners are known to cause gas, bloating, and dull skin. No thanks!

All that prepping and planning has paid off and now it's time to just have fun with your girls and enjoy every moment of prom. Don't worry about any SNAFUS (like spilling your drink on your dress!). Solutions for every yikes style scenario are in Chapter 14.

8

GET GLOWING SKIN

You know that old acne legend about chocolate causing breakouts? Well, good news—it's totally false! (Disclaimer: There is a strong link between what you eat and how your skin looks.) To ensure your face is flawless and glowing on prom night (and every night!) top-notch dermatologist Dr. Murad has signed up to help. His celebrity fans include Rachel Zoe, Kristin Chenoweth, Dianna Agron, and Lucy Hale, and he's here to give you all the insider information you'll need for radiant, prom-ready skin that's rich in nutrients.

EATING SMART

Your perfect complexion starts on the inside. In fact, Dr. Murad says 80 percent of what your skin needs to be healthy comes from what you put into your body, while topical treatments can aid in the other 20 percent. Munch on this advice from Hollywood's favorite clear skin expert.

► During the week of prom, eat at least one whole egg each day to get your daily requirement of lecithin, a cell wall-builder. This will lead to strong, water-tight cells, which result in healthy, clear skin.

► Snack on a handful of walnuts, which contain cell-hydrating omega-3 fatty acids. Drinking water is important for your body, but you can also "eat" water. Foods like fresh fruits and veggies are composed primarily of water. A watermelon is 92 percent water and zucchini, spinach, tomato, and eggplant all have a water content of over 90 percent.

► Goji berries are another smart way to eat your way to better skin. They'll add a dose of free-radical fighting antioxidants, trace minerals, and B vitamins—all components for a beautiful glow—to your diet! Look for USDA certified goji berries at your local health store or a specialty shop.

DEALING WITH IMPERFECTIONS

Help! I have a freakishly large zit!

If you feel a zit emerging under your skin the night before prom, or wake up with a beast on your face the morning of, don't pick or squeeze it! Instead, follow Dr. Murad's 1-2-3 advice to clear that sucker up.

► **Step 1: Take out the redness.** Place crushed cucumbers directly on the pimple; it's an anti-inflammatory that will reduce the zit's redness.

► **Step 2: Stop the swelling.** Use an ice pack to calm the breakout. You can also take an internal anti-inflammatory, such as ibuprofen or aspirin, to minimize the bump.

► **Step 3: Hide the rest.** Consider concealer your best friend when a pimple gets in your way to clear skin. You want to choose one that will hide and *treat* a zit, so look for a product, like Murad's Acne Treatment Concealer, with a noncomedogenic foundation (meaning it won't clog pores) and containing salicylic acid, ascorbyl palmitate, green tea extract, and vitamin E .

Fighting Bacne

Pimples don't just pop up on your face: You can have breakouts across your chest, shoulders, and back—all areas that are difficult to hide in a prom dress. What's causing this body acne? It's likely a cocktail of clogged pores, stress, diet, and hormones, explains Dr. Murad. Fight back by showering thoroughly after workouts; sweat can easily become trapped on the skin, thereby breeding bacteria and clogging pores. Use face and body products that contain salicylic acid to help clear those pores and also exfoliate away dead skin cells. Finish by applying an oil-reducing toner after showering.

DR. MURAD'S DO'S AND DON'TS

Do: Eat foods rich in vitamin A, or you can also take a supplement. Sweet potatoes are packed with this vitamin, or you can nosh on carrots, dark leafy greens, butternut squash, or cantaloupe.

Do: Keep your stress levels in check. When you're feeling stressed, oil glands have to work that much harder, thereby creating excess oil that clogs pores. Hormones can also prompt the sebaceous glands to overproduce oil. When this oil is met with dead skin cells and bacteria—kaboom!—blackheads and pimples form.

Don't: Skimp on sleep. An overall healthy lifestyle is a vital factor in achieving clear skin. In addition to minimizing your stress, avoid exposure to pollution and keep your body well-rested. Remember, the major component of treating acne starts with a happy body.

VITAMIN A+!

While vitamin A works
wonders for your skin, it's also
pretty sweet for your nails because it
prevents them from becoming dull and
dry. Keep pampering those fingers and
toes with a luxe mani and pedi—and flip
the page to hear about at-home
spa treatment.

9

MAKEUP TIPS FROM THE PROS

Putting your makeup on perfectly is a talent (seriously!). If it doesn't come naturally now, it will soon! Start by experimenting with different looks a few days before prom so that you'll have plenty of trial and error time. The trick to transforming into the most glamorous version of yourself is to draw attention to your very best feature. For instance, do a smoky eye and faux lashes so your eyes will really stand out. Then, keep the rest of your look subtle, like wearing a nude or peach gloss. Caking on too much makeup is a major no-no because it's completely unnatural. Practice with the pro advice from beauty expert Meredith Gray, then take test photos of the looks you like most and ask your family and friends for their feedback.

MEET THE EXPERT: MEREDITH GRAY

Meredith first discovered her love of beauty products at age five when she became fascinated by her grandmother's multilayered skincare and makeup routine. She took her passion for beauty and writing to several magazines, most notably *Seventeen*, where she was beauty editor. She now works in global education for Estée Lauder, and it's her personal mission to help women of all ages look and feel their prettiest every day.

PERFECT SKIN

Prep your pores for their close-up!

- ► **Step 1: Wash your face.** Use a gentle cleanser, dry your face, and then apply an oil-free moisturizer. Let that sit for a minute or two, and then apply a primer. Using a primer creates a smooth surface so your foundation goes on evenly, and it will ensure that your makeup lasts all through prom night!

- ► **Step 2: Find the right concealer.** Choose the type of coverage you want, ranging from heavy to light. Liquid foundations provide the maximum coverage, powders give your skin a matte look, and tinted moisturizers give a light, dewy finish.

  Avoid applying liquid foundation all over—that creates a cakey look. Instead, use a foundation brush or sponge. Only apply your foundation where you need it—or any place where you have redness or an uneven skin tone, such as around your nose, on your forehead, and along your jawline. Blend to make everything even, and run the foundation down your neck to avoid that telltale makeup line along your jaw!

- ► **Step 3: Brighten your complexion.** If you were too excited to sleep and woke up with dark circles under your eyes, fake a fresh face by applying a concealer one shade lighter than your foundation to this delicate area. A concealer with a light pink base works best because it cancels out darkness and brightens your entire eye area.

  Apply the concealer lightly to your eyes, as if you're creating goggles. You'll want to cover your lids and the half-circles below your eyes, as well as the side of your nose next to your eyes, and even along your brow bones. Then blend, blend, blend!

► **Step 4: Add a warm glow.** When using bronzer, keep in mind that a little goes a long way. Powder formulas are the easiest to use since they allow you to build up to your desired shade. Use a big, fluffy brush to sweep the bronzer across all the points where the sun would naturally hit your face—your forehead, the bridge of your nose, and your chin. You can also add some along your temples and jawline, too, for soft contours.

BEGINNING TO END SKIN SECRETS

Before You Start: The night before prom (or any big event), apply your favorite mask so your skin is squeaky clean. It will make a huge difference in how smoothly your makeup goes on.

When Applying: Makeup products containing SPF are great for daytime use to protect your skin, but some can do an unwanted dance with camera flashes, resulting in your face having that ghostly, white-all-over look. Consider investing in a separate concealer for events where you'll be saying a lot of cheeses!

The Final Step: Set your makeup with a loose, translucent powder after you've finished applying everything. This will keep your handiwork in place, and you can use it throughout the night to blot out unwanted shine.

How to use concealer to disguise a zit: Apply your foundation first, and then take a small, rounded concealer brush and dab the cover-up on your zit. Using your ring finger, lightly tap the makeup into your skin. You may need to repeat this several times in order to get the right amount of coverage. Lastly, set the concealer with a light dusting of loose powder in the same shade as your foundation. *Sayonara*, acne!

COLORFUL CHEEKS

You can use a highlighter, bronzer, or blush—or any combination of the three!—for pretty cheekbones.

What Shade is Best for Me?

Follow Meredith's suggestions for your ideal color combo:

Fair skin: Your tone matches best with cool, pink shades that complement your natural rosiness.

Beige skin: Peachy colors look amazing on you because they have warm yellow-hued undertones.

Olive skin: You want purple-based pink shades to counteract the hints of green in your skin.

Vanessa Hudgens opts for a more natural look by applying blush lightly over the apples of her cheeks.

Golden skin: Cool peach shades with silvery undertones are the perfect complement to your already warm skin, making it totally radiant.

Bronze skin: Tawny and copper shades are perfect for you because they accentuate your skin's naturally pink undertones. Opt for reddish, brick-toned pinks to bring the glam. These hues are a subtle way to feature a pop of color.

How to Apply

For a natural look, take a big, fluffy brush and dust the blush onto the apples of your cheeks, then sweep it out toward your hairline and slightly up toward your temples.

EYE MAKEUP

Curl your lashes first, and then create a fierce statement.

What Colors Should I Wear?

Choose the shades that will make your eyes pop!

Light Eyes: Blue and green eyes look great with earthy shades like taupe and gray. Really want to amp up your color? Try hunter green shades if you have green eyes, and wear mauve shades with blue eyes.

Dark Eyes: Brown and hazel-eyed girls can draw attention to their peeps with gold and peach shades. For more intensity, go for a purple or violet shadow.

Gold shadow can be both dramatic and subtle. Actress Sharon Leal creates a polished, natural look by pairing it with peachy blush and gloss.

Using Liner and Mascara

Opt for dark brown or gray liners because black can look harsh. However, classic black is always best for mascara! Apply two coats to top lashes only for a flirty, lush look. (Mascara on your lower lashes is more likely to run, giving you raccoon eyes later in the night!)

How to Wear Faux Lashes

Lash strips are your best bet because those are the easiest to use.

Hunger Games actress Jennifer Lawrence amplifies the drama with winged shadow and fantastic, long lashes.

► **Step 1:** Position the strips along your lash line before adding the glue, advises Meredith, so that you can trim the edges to fit your eye shape if necessary. It's easiest if you look *down* into a mirror, rather than straight ahead. (For example, use a hand mirror and place it flat on your desk.) This helps guide your sight line so you're sure to apply the strip evenly.

► **Step 2:** Squeeze a small amount of glue onto the back of your hand. (Don't apply it directly to the strip!) Give it a few seconds to become tacky, then gently drag the strip across the back of your hand, through the glue.

► **Step 3:** To place the strip on your eye, stick it down in the center of your lid, then gently guide each end to follow your eye shape. Hold your eye closed for at least fifteen seconds, then carefully open your eye and make sure the lashes feel comfortable. It may take a couple of tries to get it just right!

CREATE THE PERFECT SMOKY EYE IN 5 STEPS!

If you're doing an intense, smoky eye look, rearrange the steps for doing your makeup. Meredith advises to apply your primer all over first, but then skip ahead to your eye makeup so you can wipe away any shadow smudges or mascara smears before applying foundation.

Step 1: Begin with a light, shimmery champagne-colored shadow, and apply that all over your lid, from the lash line up to the brow bone. Add some to the inner corners of your eyes, too, to give them extra sparkle.

Step 2: Pick an eyeshadow duo that has complementary shades of slate gray or chocolate brown—one shade should be darker than the other. Starting with the darker shade, apply it to the outside corner of your eye from lash line to crease, but stop when you reach the middle of your eye (right above your pupil).

Step 3: With the lighter shade of the duo, use the technique from Step 2, this time starting from the inner corner of your eye and blending toward the middle. Important: Make sure to blend really well so you don't see a line between the two shades!

Step 4: Next, line your upper lash line with a pencil liner in a shade that matches your shadow. (Avoid pure black since it tends to look harsh in photos.) Line as close to your lash line as possible. Do the same on your lower lash line, carefully running the pencil along the inner rim of your eyes.

Step 5: Last, apply a black, volumizing mascara. Wiggle the wand back and forth at the base of your lashes to make them look fuller, then run the wand out toward the tips. Apply two coats on top lashes and one on the bottom lashes. Clean up any accidental mascara smudges around your eyes with a cotton swab, and pack extra in your purse to touch up mascara that runs during the night.

Selena Gomez sports smoky eyes in shades of silver and black. Experiment with different color combinations to find your favorite look!

SMOOCHABLE LIPS

Softening your pout

Gently rub your lips first using a dry toothbrush; this will loosen flakes and create a smooth base. Apply a balm, let that sink in, then top with the color of your choice.

Shades to try for prom

Now is the time to go totally glam, but you still want to look like yourself! If you're hesitant about wearing a bright shade, don't attempt it for the first time on prom night. Why? Because you want to feel fully confident, which in turn, makes you look

Get a romantic look like *Twilight's* Ashley Greene with a light coral or rose shade.

QUICK TIP!

Make Your Lips Look Fuller!

Apply a light-colored (pink or berry) stain first, then top with a gloss. Next, take a gold-colored shadow and pat a little bit onto your cupid's bow at the top of your lips and a little bit onto the center of your bottom lip. This draws light toward the plumpest parts of your lips, making them appear fuller overall.

your absolute best! Light pinks and peaches are always flattering for every skin tone, and sheer berry is a trendy, fun shade.

Applying lipstick

Fill your lips in with a nude-colored lip liner first—this gives the lipstick something to stick to so it lasts. You don't want to line around your mouth with the nude lip liner because that will look too harsh. Use a lip brush to apply the color since it gives you more control for the most precise application.

Other Options

Glosses are easy to wear and reapply. Many brands also make lip crayons now, which are similar to a gloss and stain in one, so they give a hint of color while also adding shine.

If you're bold and fun like Emma Stone, why not try bright red lips? Test a few different shades of red to find one that you like, and pair it with neutral colored eye shadow.

YOUR GUIDE TO PERFECT EYEBROWS

You can't forget about your brows on prom night! They frame your face and give off a polished look that draws attention to your pretty eyes. Top celebrity brow specialist Elke Von Freudenberg has put her magic shaping touch on everyone in Hollywood from Kate Moss to James Franco. Now it's your turn. Take this advice straight from Elke for magazine cover worthy brows!

WHEN SHOULD I TWEEZE OR WAX?

Both should be done one or two days before prom so any redness or swelling will be gone before the big day!

Tweezing

Hairs pull out easiest when they're tweezed right after a hot shower. You can also steam your face to relax pores. Use a witch hazel toner both before and after tweezing to avoid breakouts, and avoid applying heavy creams, oils, or foundations for at least three or four hours.

When tweezing, always pull in the direction of the hair growth. This removes the "ouch" factor when pulling. Keep the skin tight by holding it down with two fingers as you pull. Tweezing doesn't cause pain—it's the skin moving that hurts. By preventing the skin from moving, you remove the sting.

Waxing

Opt for a honey-based wax when removing hair at home; it comes off with water so any excess wax can be easily removed. First, apply a light layer of cortisone cream followed by a light layer of baby powder to protect your skin. Test that the wax is a comfortable temperature by putting a small amount on the inside of your wrist. For the most precise removal, do smaller sections at a time rather than one large one so you're controlling the amount of hair pulled out.

Miranda Cosgrove's brows are polished while still looking natural.

HOW SHOULD I SHAPE MY BROWS?

The beginning of your brow can start anywhere between the bridge of your nose to right above the tear duct of your eye. To be on the safe side, start the brow line either at the bridge of the nose or halfway between the bridge of the nose and the tear duct. Any further in can cause the nose to look too wide, and any further out can make the eyes appear close set!

The highest arch of your eyebrow should hit directly above the outer corner of the iris of your eye. The end of your brows should be where an invisible diagonal line from the outer corner of your nose to the outer corner of the eye would land.

HOW DO I USE A BROW PENCIL OR BROW SHADOW?

Choose a color that's one or two shades lighter than your brow color. (This will make blending the color into the brow much easier!) Start by applying your shadow or pencil along the bottom of the brow in short

Blake Lively pairs her high rounded arch with a touch of highlight shadow.

strokes. Then, take a spoolie or mascara wand and brush the color upward into the brow. Blending like this mimics the natural look of the brow being darker at the roots and lighter at the ends of hairs.

HOW DO I AVOID OVER-PLUCKING?

Only pluck obvious stray hairs that are underneath and between the brows. Avoid plucking the top of brows because before you know it you can remove too much, resulting in a flat brow with no arches. You're aiming for a cleaned up version of your brow—not to completely change it.

Who cares about being a prom queen when you've just been nominated for most beautiful? Have fun testing out different combinations, like a bright red lip and neutral shadow, or a smoky eye and pale pink gloss. Your options are endless! Just keep in mind that makeup should draw attention to your best features, not overwhelm your face. After all, natural beauty has the most sparkle!

QUICK TIP!

A shimmering highlight shadow under the entire brow makes brow lines look stronger, especially in photos! Also, use a brow gel to tame fine and thin brow hairs; a clear brow wax will keep coarser, thicker hairs in place.

10

HAIRSTYLES YOU CAN DO

Who says you need to pay a professional to have a stunning hairstyle on prom night? With a little practice, these six styles provided by Pam Kelly, Senior Director of National Technical Education for Fantastic Sam's Hair Salons (they have over 1,200 salons across the country!) will give you ooh-la-la hair—no appointment required. Choose one style for prom, another for the following Friday night, another for the Saturday after that, and after that . . . well, you get the picture.

QUICK TIP!

HAIROLOGY 101
Get the scoop on the products required for these promtastic hairstyles.

1. Blow-out serums are used to add shine and smoothness to your hair. Choose one that contains silicone for the best result.

2. Thermal guards form a heat barrier that protects your hair from breakage caused by hot tools, like a curling iron or blow-dryer. Make sure the label clearly states that it prevents heat damage.

3. As a finishing touch, spray hair with a light to medium hold hairspray so tresses still have a natural texture.

THE SLEEK AND STRAIGHT BLOWOUT

This style has a chic, retro vibe!

Ideal hair length: Past the shoulders.

Most flattering for: Round faces benefit from this look because it elongates the face.

Makeup to match: Light, soft shades from a neutral color palette.

How to do it:

►**Step 1:** Keep your hair frizz-free by shampooing and conditioning with a moisturizing formula.

►**Step 2:** While hair is still wet, apply a blow-out serum that contains silicone or argan oil; it will give your tresses extra shine and smoothness.

Actress Dakota Fanning pairs her long, shiny tresses with soft make-up.

►**Step 3:** Blow-dry using a paddle brush to keep your hair close to your scalp. Use the nozzle on the blow-dryer to focus heat directly on the strands you are drying. Always point the blow-dryer down in the direction the hair grows to add shine.

►**Step 4:** Once your locks are dry, part your hair down the center of your scalp. (Psst: A center part draws attention to your eyes!)

►**Step 5:** Hold everything in place with a light mist of hairspray.

CURLY AND ROMANTIC DOWN-DO

Get playful with this hairstyle that's perfect for medium and long hair!

Ideal hair length: Medium to long.

Most flattering for: This style softens the angular lines of rectangle and square faces.

Makeup to match: Light pink and rose shades.

Use a large barrel curling iron to get loose curls like Taylor Swift. Complete the look with rosy cheeks and pretty pink lipstick.

How to do it:

► **Step 1:** First, shampoo and condition with a moisturizing formula. Next, protect yourself! Apply a thermal guard spray to your tresses to prevent damage caused by heat from the blow-dryer and curling iron.

► **Step 2:** Use a round brush while blow-drying to add fullness and volume.

► **Step 3:** When you're done drying your hair, make a deep side part.

► **Step 4:** Leave the hair above your ears flat, and add volume and curls below. Choose a curling iron that will give you the size curls you want: the smaller the barrel of the iron, the tighter and smaller the curls. Curl one to two inch sections of hair at a time and then let the curls cool for five minutes.

► **Step 5:** Using your fingers only (no combs or brushes!), rake through the curls until they loosely fall into your desired style.

► **Step 6:** Finish by spraying a light hairspray to hold everything in place.

 Your part should begin at the highest point of your eyebrow, this will flatter your face shape the most.

GRECIAN BRAID

This look is more elaborate and adds drama to your prom vibe!

Ideal hair length: Shoulder length or longer.

Most flattering for: All! This style opens your eyes and cheekbone areas.

Makeup to match: Go for a bold red lip, but balance with far less intense eye makeup.

How to do it:

► **Step 1:** Start by washing and conditioning your hair. Protect those pretty tresses from heat damage by applying a thermal guard spray before blow-drying.

► **Step 2:** Once you've finished blow-drying, divide your hair into two sections, separating the front of the head from the back. The first section will be temporarily placed on the top of your head and the second section pulled into a ponytail at the back of the head toward the back crown area.

QUICK TIP!

How Do I Backcomb My Hair??

Hold a one-inch section of hair straight out from the scalp, Pam instructs. Using a comb on the backside of the section, place the teeth of the comb halfway into the section and lightly comb the hair down toward the root. Keep doing this movement until a "pillow" of hair forms at the base of your head.

► **Step 3:** Now go back to the hair in the top section and divide that into two sections across the top of the head. Section one will be closest to your forehead and section two directly behind it. Take section two and backcomb to create volume. After backcombing, lightly comb the hair into the back crown area and pin loose hair into the base of the ponytail with bobby pins.

Make this look your own. Try playing with the position of the braid or tie the back section into a loose bun instead of a ponytail. If you have curly hair, no need to backcomb! Let the natural volume of your curls do the work for you.

► **Step 4:** In the very front (section one), create a deep side part. Just behind this area, take a two-inch strand of hair and braid. Then, take the braid and sweep it over the top of your head to behind the ear. Secure into the base of the ponytail with a bobby pin. Sweep the remaining area behind your part in the same direction of the braid and secure over the ear with a bobby pin.

► **Step 5:** Now move back to the ponytail and curl individual strands in a loose wave. Tousle lightly with your fingers and spray a mist of hairspray to hold everything in place.

FLIRTY CHIGNON

A classic chignon is glamour done simply! Because this style pulls hair away from your face, this 'do works best when wearing extra-fancy earrings.

Ideal hair length: Chin length and longer.

Most flattering for: All! Sweeping hair back highlights your pretty facial features.

Makeup to match: Since the style is very simple yet classic, makeup can be more dramatic, such as a smoky eye.

Amanda Seyfried wears a variation of the flirty chignon. Try it for yourself! Instead of back-combing your hair, tie it into a low ponytail and move on to step 4.

How to do it:

▶ **Step 1:** Shampoo and condition your hair, then apply a thermal guard spray and blow-out serum to protect your hair from heat damage while adding shine.

▶ **Step 2:** Blow-dry, then take the top crown area and lightly backcomb to create a soft "pillow," or added volume.

▶ **Step 3:** Pull your tresses into a ponytail and secure at the back of the head, being sure not to flatten the "pillow." If you do accidentally, a simple fix is to take the tail from a tail comb and pull the hair on the crown up.

▶ **Step 4:** Take your ponytail and brush it smooth. Lightly roll the ponytail under at the nape of your neck, secure with a bobby pin or two—this will form the chignon. Tame flyaways with a light hairspray and viola!

QUICK TIP!

Pam says to use bobby pins that match your hair color so they'll stay easily hidden throughout the night. You can add instant glam to your look with rhinestone or jeweled hairpins. For a sweeter touch, pin the stem of silk or fresh flowers into your hairstyle after applying hairspray.

GLAM SIDE PONYTAIL

This style is effortlessly cute!

Ideal hair length: Shoulder length or longer.

Most flattering for: All! (But flirty personalities match this fun look!)

Makeup to match: All color palettes work well with this style; if your dress is very detailed, wear soft colors. Otherwise, amp up your look with a bold lip or strong eye makeup.

Actress Keke Palmer keeps it fun and flirty by curling two sections of hair instead of twisting them together.

How to do it:

► **Step 1:** Shampoo and condition, then protect your hair from heat damage by applying a thermal guard. Next, keep your tresses shiny by using a blow-out serum.

► **Step 2:** Using a brush, blow-dry (remember to always keep the blow-dryer pointed down in the direction hair grows) and then brush your hair into a low ponytail off to the side.

► **Step 3:** Take the ponytail and divide into two sections; twist the sections loosely together. Secure at the ends of the twisted sections with a small rubber band.

► **Step 4:** Using your fingers, softly separate the ponytail to create a loose yet tousled effect.

► **Step 5:** Spray lightly with hairspray.

SWEPT BUN UP-DO

This classy look works best with longer hair and dramatic makeup!

Ideal hair length: Medium to long.

Most flattering for: Since the hair is lifted up, it works well on round faces because you're giving the illusion of more length.

Makeup to match: Play up your best feature with this look. Love your eyes? Apply faux lashes and a darker eye shadow.

For a classy but playful look, try a low side bun like Emma Roberts and top it off with a fun headband.

How to do it:

► **Step 1:** Shampoo, condition, and blow-dry. Apply a thermal guard product to protect your hair from heat damage and a blow-out serum to add shine.

► **Step 2:** Pull your hair into a ponytail on the top of your head and secure with a elastic band.

► **Step 3:** To create a bun, take the ponytail, twist and roll the hair around the base of the ponytail, and secure with several bobby pins.

► **Step 4:** You can secure the ponytail at different areas of your head to achieve different looks: up high for maximum drama, down low for a subdued look, on the side for a funky twist. Add a special touch with a sparkle headband.

► **Step 5:** Spray lightly with hairspray to secure the look.

11

NAILING IT

Knowing how to do your own manicure and pedicure will save you tons (TONS!) of money throughout your life. Keep practicing the steps below with a steady hand and (shh!) no one will ever know you *didn't* have your nails done at a salon.

DO YOUR OWN MANICURE:

► **Step 1:** Remove any polish already on your nails and then file them. For an oval shape, file from the corner of your nails into the center with an emery board. For square ends, move the board horizontally in one direction.

► **Step 2:** Using a buffer block, lightly go back and forth over the top of your nails to smooth them.

► **Step 3:** If needed, take hangnail scissors and remove any unwanted skin around the nail.

► **Step 4:** Apply a liquid cuticle remover to soften your cuticles, wait one minute, and then let your hands rest in a bowl of warm water for a few minutes.

► **Step 5:** Dry your hands and use a cuticle pusher to gently push back each cuticle.

► **Step 6:** Apply a clear base coat. Slightly tilt your hand toward you so you can properly get all sides of the nail.

► **Step 7:** Stroke your colored polish down each nail with your hand still slightly tilted. Apply two coats and swipe the brush across the bottom of your nail when you've finished to prevent chipping.

► **Step 8:** Next, apply a clear top coat, which will also prevent chipping and add shine.

► **Step 9:** Let dry.

DO YOUR OWN PEDICURE:

► **Step 1:** Start by removing any polish already on your toes.

► **Step 2:** Fill your tub with warm water—just enough to soak your feet—and pour in a few scoops of Epsom salt. Let your toes rest in the water for five minutes.

► **Step 3:** Exfoliate the bottom of your feet by gently moving a pumice stone or foot filer back and forth. Rinse and dry.

► **Step 4:** Use hangnail scissors if necessary to remove any damaged skin around nail.

► **Step 5:** Apply a liquid cuticle remover to soften your cuticles. Wait a minute or two and then gently push back cuticles with a cuticle pusher.

► **Step 6:** Clip your nails straight across or file them using an emery board.

► **Step 7:** Take a buffer block and swipe it back and forth across the top of your nails to smooth them. Thoroughly rinse your feet and dry.

► **Step 8:** Place toe separators on each foot. (You can also weave a paper towel or toilet paper in and out of your toes as an alternative.)

► **Step 9:** Just like a manicure, apply a clear base coat first.

► **Step 10:** Next, apply two coats of your colored polish and swipe the brush across the bottom of each nail to prevent chipping.

► **Step 11:** Finish with a clear top coat and let dry.

TREAT YOURSELF!

Once you've taken the time to pamper your fingers and toes, don't let the party end there. Use the tricks below to turn your at-home mani-pedi into a full-on spa day!

Make Your Own Perfume!

Paris Hilton and Kim Kardashian aren't the only girls who can bottle up their own signature scent! Celebrity aromatherapist Adora Winquist tells you how to mix and match until you've created a truly unique blend that's all yours!

What You'll Need:

► One .33 ounce roll-on bottle or other perfume bottle in a similar size

► Organic jojoba oil

► About five different essential oils

Key Aromatherapy Oils: Visit your local health food store and scour their essential oils collection. Hold about five bottles together at a time and inhale to see how the scents harmonize. Keep experimenting until you find your perfect blend!

► Blood Orange: vibrant and uplifting

► Lemon: confident and clear

► Jasmine Absolute: mysterious and inspirational

A list of my
Favorite Scents

_____

_____

_____

► Rose: hopeful

► Patchouli: grounding and balancing

► Sandalwood: tranquil and supportive

► Neroli: bright and carefree

► Geranium: powerful and feminine

► Lime : zesty and bright

► Lavender: calming

► Ylang Ylang : sweet and beautiful

► Frankincense: peaceful

► Vanilla: warm and spicy

► Bergamot: fresh and joyful

Once you've selected your oils, mix a combination of twenty-two drops total into your base of organic jojoba. It may take a few practice runs to perfect your blend, so jot down each recipe to keep track. (Psst: Making your family and friends their own perfume is a great idea for presents, too!)

Notes

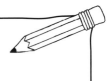

Notes

Notes

Part

PROM NIGHT

The big night is finally here! There's so much excitement swirling around, but you're probably feeling a little anxious, too, right? That's totally normal. The hour-by-hour calendar starting on page 68 will keep you on schedule, and exercises from celebrity trainer on page 44 will calm any pre-dance jitters.

Plus, this section will equip you with everything you need to solve those freak-out moments, like what to do if—gasp!—you accidentally stain your dress. Mimi Kaupe, a costume designer for ABC Family, walks you through removing spills, repairing rips, and more, so (phew!) breathe a sigh of relief.

Now, back to the fun! Don't let the party end with the last dance— throw an awesome post-prom bash at your place for you and your besties. Serve up three splashy mocktails with the recipes in Chapter 13, and follow the directions for setting up a candy bar or creating your own dance floor right in the middle of your living room! Yup, your friends' jaws will hit the floor. Keep them in awe until the very last moment by sending them home with sweet goodie bags. (After a party *this* fun, don't be surprised if you're practically forced to be on next year's prom planning committee!)

12

HOSTING A PRE-PROM PARTY

Get the party started early! If you have to go from one friend's living room to another in order to take group photos, you'll wind up wasting precious prom night moments (and upping the odds that your limo driver will get lost!). Instead, take your prom experience to the next level by staging your own photo shoot at home and throwing a chic shindig to kick off the night in style!

HOW TO CREATE A PROM PHOTO BACKDROP

(Don't forget to smile—these are the photos you'll look at forever!)

Option 1: Celebrity party planner Debi Lilly—who's even thrown swanky affairs for Oprah!—suggests creating a focal point for group photos by taping dozens of long, vertical crepe paper streamers to a wall. If it's a beautiful day, take the picture party outside by clipping the streamers to a clothesline.

THE DO'S AND DON'TS...
Capturing the Night!

DO: Take short videos throughout the entire night on your phone and camera!

DO: Only post non-questionable photos from prom night on Twitter, Facebook, and other social media sites. Besides your parents, colleges or future employers might be watching!

DON'T: Pose for photos directly under a light—that will cast a shadow under your eyes. Beauty no-no!

Option 2: Another cool idea is to tape two rectangular plastic tablecloths side-by-side to your wall, stapling a festive garland to the sides, and adding bunches of latex balloons filled with helium on either side. Purchase two weights to hold the balloons in place, or paint a large rock—you want it to look pretty in photos! Then, hang latex balloons upside down from the ceiling (securing them with just a bit of tape on the ends of the string). These should hit a few inches above your head and fall at different lengths. Choose bold colors for a photo op bursting with pre-prom excitement!

> ### DID YOU KNOW?
>
> Leaning to the right probably flatters you the most, according to a study published in *Experimental Brain Research*. Why is this the case? Because you tend to show more emotion on your left side—think wider eyes and a bigger smile. And happiness like that is always an attractive quality!

Option 3: Get as creative as possible with your photo backdrop; order four jumbo letter balloons that spell PROM. Tie their ribbons to four weights with the letters spaced evenly and approximately six feet off the ground (unless someone's date is really tall!) and pose in front.

LAY OUT THE RED CARPET

Or the purple carpet. Or any color you want! Wow your friends from the very first moment they arrive! A roll of inexpensive cotton, or three to five yards of felt, will cost less than twenty dollars, Debi says. Securely tape down both ends of the fabric using non-damaging colored masking tape. Just add paparazzi for the full Hollywood treatment.

MOVING INSIDE: MUSIC AND DECORATIONS

Set the mood

A great playlist will get everyone's energy up! Download twenty or so of your favorite fast songs and keep the playlist on loop throughout the night. Play with lighting, too, to flip your home into a party atmosphere. Color light bulbs create a fun effect.

Choose a two-color scheme!

Decorate with one really bold color that reflects your excitement (like hot pink), and one that's a bit more subdued (like a softer white). For an extra splash, order a few dozen helium balloons in those colors and scatter them around the room, letting the long strings dangle down. Scatter matching confetti on tabletops for a finishing touch.

FOOD AND DRINKS

Keep it light—you don't want to feel full when you hit the dance floor!

Set up a snack station

Chips and dip, anyone? Here's an easy party hit from Debi's treasure chest: Pour tortilla chips into a bowl, and place next to bowls of black beans, shredded cheese, corn, salsas (label mild, medium, and spicy), and guacamole. Have appetizer plates on hand and plenty of napkins. Another option is asking a parent to pass around hot, easy-to-make hors d'oeuvres—like pigs in a blanket or mini-pretzels—on a pretty platter for an extra swanky touch.

Serve Fun Drinks

Create a signature drink for your party! A simple lemonade mix gets a luxe makeover when it's served in chic stemware. Check out places like IKEA and Pier 1 for inexpensive ideas. Top with fresh fruit or mini umbrellas to add a festive pop of color to your drink.

Photos You Absolutely Have to Take on Prom Night

▶ A posed and candid photo with your date.

▶ A posed and candid photo with your friends.

▶ A zoomed-in photo of your flowers.

▶ A zoomed-in photo of your heels.

▶ Your dress hanging on a hanger.

▶ You, getting your hair and makeup done.

▶ You, turned around, showing the back of your dress and hair.

▶ A headshot after your hair and makeup are done.

▶ Your date seeing you for the first time.

▶ You with your siblings alone, and one with your date.

▶ You with your parents alone, and one with your date.

▶ A photo of you with your prom group.

▶ A silly photo from inside your ride.

▶ A candid photo of you dancing with your date and a candid shot busting a move with friends.

▶ If you're a couple, a smooching photo with your date.

▶ A photo with your BFFs at dinner and the after-party.

TEEN TALK

"Look at old photos to see which angle you like best on yourself. Never stand straight in front of the camera—you always want to lean sideways a little to make yourself look more flattering. Also, I never put my arms straight down beside me."

—Caitlin Beadles, age 17
Arlanta, Georgia

13

KEEP THE PARTY GOING

Ready for the next round? The fun won't fade when you host a fab after-party! (Warning: With these tips, you may even one-up the dance!) Start by dimming the lights to set a post-prom mood. (Strobe light, anyone?) While the pre-party is all about getting your energy level up, now it's time to kick off the heels and recap the dance's highlights with your friends. Get a hot playlist on loop, follow the tips below, and wait for those "'Awesome party!'" compliments to come rolling in!

SET THE ATMOSPHERE

The right decorations can turn your living room into an after-hours club!

Greet your guests with crazy party props

Start and end your bash with cool surprises. Pass out silly goodies to get everyone pumped. Inflatable guitars, colorful leis, oversized neon shades, feather boas—the possibilities are endless! Check out affordable party sites like OrientalTrading.com for deals and steals.

Section off a dance floor

Tell your friends to throw a pair of flip-flops in their ride, so now they can kick off their heels and really dance! Square off an area for the dance floor by hanging streamers from the ceiling. You can also blow up balloons or fill them with helium and scatter around the area for an extra festive touch.

Transform furniture

Throw matching colored sheets over large pieces of furniture to create a loungy vibe. Continue the living room transformation by temporarily removing photos and artwork from the room. If you have an old frame lying around that's large enough for two people's faces, paint it and add silly decorations. Then pass it around during the party for people to pose with. You can create an entire Facebook album devoted solely to these shots.

At the end of the night, hand out goodie bags

To go that extra mile, give your friends a gift when it's time to (finally!) call it a night. Purchase goodie bags that you can fill with bright tissue paper—presentation is everything! Check your local party store for inexpensive fillers, or you can really take your bag to the next level by pre-ordering a personalized gift, like a frame, stationery, or pens. Everyone will walk away raving about your bash!

AWESOME ACTIVITIES

Besides chatting and dancing (and dancing some more!), squeeze these other activity ideas into your night for some extra memories.

Elect your own king and queen!

This royalty ballot is meant to be more silly than serious. Create a ballot for your friends to fill out and drop into a box (take an old shoebox, cut a slit on top for dropping ballots into, and use wrapping paper to decorate). Of course, you'll need creative crowns for your king and queen, so just scope out the local party store.

Play prom idol!

Beverly Hills event planner Deborah Kattler Kupetz hits a party high note with this idea. If you make karaoke interactive, your friends—even those with less than Carrie Underwood caliber pipes—will want to join in. Pass out index cards labeled *Yes* and *No* to vote on the songs people will sing. Appoint three judges to decide whether each singer advances to the next round. It really doesn't matter how well someone can sing; it's about how much fun they're having! Get your friends to loosen up and leave their comfort zone by passing out crazy wigs and other wild props.

FESTIVE SNACKS AND DRINKS

You already ate dinner, so now cater to your friends' sweet teeth.

Set up a candy bar

Tired from dancing all night? Time for a sugar rush! Buy candy bags and scoopers, as well as your favorite sweet tooth treats. For a pro touch, make a few stacks using wide books—different heights—on top of a table and throw a tablecloth on top. Then, place the candy in bowls on top of the stacks for a tiered effect.

Try these (easy!) mocktail recipes

Rename these classic drinks something that has special meaning to your group and serve in fancy glassware for a chic touch!

Mocktail Champagne:
2 liters of apple cider
2 liters of ginger ale
Just pour these together in a large bowl and add ice.

Shirley Temple:
2 liters of lemon-lime soda
2 liters of ginger ale
Add a splash of grenadine syrup to taste.
Maraschino cherries make every drink more fun!
Add to individual glasses freely.

Virgin Piña Colada:
Add three parts pineapple juice and one part coconut cream.
Mix with ice in a blender.
Place a wedge of pineapple on the side of each glass.

As one last surprise for your friends, snap a group photo wearing your crazy props and silly crowns. Print those out over the weekend and slip the pictures into their lockers first thing on Monday morning. Just don't be surprised when the prom committee recruits you for next year!

FIVE OTHER AWESOME POST-PROM IDEAS!

1. **Go bowling.** Because really, when else will you get to bowl in a gown?

2. **Go roller skating!** Move the party from the dance floor to the rink and create more special memories with your friends.

3. **Check out a comedy show.** This is one way to keep the laughs rolling all night!

4. **Keep dancing at an all-ages club.** It will feel like prom never ended.

5. **Throw a midnight pool party!** Use your backyard—or a friend's—to stretch the night a little longer. Play some music (not too loud so your neighbors don't freak) and splash around with your best buds.

14

STAYING SAFE AND SANE

Wouldn't it be great if you could stash a magic wand in your purse during prom night? Unfortunately, magic wands are the stuff of fairy tales, but you have the next best thing in Mimi Kaupe—a top-notch style expert who's currently the Costume Designer for ABC Family's *The Lying Game*. (She also made every single one of her own prom dresses!)

WARDROBE MALFUNCTIONS

Thanks to Mimi, even these four major fashion nightmares can't spoil your time at the dance!

What if my dress rips?

Ask your school's custodial employees for duct tape—DJ might even have some. Cut the tape into small pieces (it's extra sticky!) using the cuticle scissors in your purse. Push the fabric back into place and tape together from the inside of your dress.

My zipper broke . . . Now what?

Take out your safety pin and cuticle scissors. First try pulling your zipper all the way down and back up. If that doesn't do the trick, pull the zipper back down and remove the bottom few teeth on the left side. Next, carefully reintroduce the teeth into the left side of the zipper and hopefully they'll align with new partners. Now, from the inside of your dress, safety pin the end of the zipper where you worked to prevent it from slipping all the way down. If all else fails, use your extra safety pins to secure the dress (and remember to pin from the inside)!

My dress doesn't fit and I don't have time to alter it. Help!

If you slip into your dress and there's too much room, try a different bra with more padding to fill it out. If you have the opposite problem and it's too snug, you can go without a bra if your dress provides enough support—but only if you're 110 percent certain it won't slip while you're dancing! Another alternative is using a "cutlet," which provides support in the front without more fabric in the back. Slimming undergarments like Spanx can also help a tight fit feel more comfortable.

TIPS FOR REMOVING EVERY KIND OF STAIN

All of your uh-oh moments are totally fixable with Mimi's advice. (Phew!) Check out the tips on the next page for ways to eliminate some of the most common stains.

Sweat Marks

Crush an aspirin, add it to room temperature water, and blot. The salicylic acid of the aspirin will dissolve the minerals left behind by evaporated sweat.

Blood

Sprinkle table salt on the stain. Blot and dry. Here's a science style fact: Salt breaks down hemoglobin in the blood, which binds stains to the fabric.

Chocolate

Dip your napkin in warm water mixed with a small amount of clear soap and blot. This will erase the oil and dye in chocolate from your dress.

Gum on Your Dress

Hold an ice cube on both sides of the fabric. The cold will "freeze" the gum so you can peel it off.

OTHER DRAMAS SOLVED!

If your date gets sick . . .

Ugh, this is a bummer—but the bright side is that you'll *still* have an awesome time at prom. You can call up a guy friend and ask for a major I-owe-you favor or text another friend who you already know was planning to go solo. Even better—join friends planning to go as a group so you can stick together during the slow songs. In the morning, show your sweet side by remembering to text your date and ask how he's feeling.

If you get sick . . .

Unfortunately, you can't plan ahead for illness, but you can make the most of such bad luck. Plan for your girls to get all decked out and go midnight bowling the next weekend; they'll love any excuse to wear their dresses again! When it comes down to it, the most important thing about prom is feeling special and having a blast with your best friends— and thankfully that's not tough to recreate!

REAL TALK

How to Deal With Friends Who
Want to Get Drunk

"It's obvious that kids are going to drink at prom, or any party at this age and grade. All you have to do is be smart and if you really do not want to do something that everyone else is doing, like drinking or smoking, all you have to do is say no. Nobody will tell you're not cool; they will actually respect your decision because at this age they are hopefully mature enough to understand. If they don't, they are not your real friends."

—Andreea Sincan, age 17
Sherman Oaks, California

If your limo arrives super late . . .

Flip back to your notes and call the after-hours manager once your driver is officially 10 minutes late. If your driver is more than 25 minutes late, it's time to put your backup plan into action so you don't waste any more time. Call the family member or friend who you kept on speed dial for such an emergency and ask them to take you to prom. Inform the manager that the driver is to now meet you at prom and you expect a price adjustment for your major inconvenience. The best thing is to have a parent handle it from here. They can get the new price in writing from the manager while you're enjoying your night!

STAYING SAFE

Prom is supposed to be a magical time, but the truth is that it has potential to turn scary, fast. You may be surrounded by everything from peer pressure to pushy dates looking to take you out of your comfort zone. Fingers crossed, you'll never face any of these sketchy situations but you should still be prepared just in case. Prom should be a night you'll never forget—not one that you wish you could!

Make a pact with your parents

Parents are parents and they're going to worry about you on prom night—especially if you're spending the night away from home or headed to post-prom parties. To calm their concerns (and score yourself a later curfew!) keep communication open. Promise to send them a quick text once an hour after the dance ends just to say you're okay. Sure, it's a pain, but don't forget to do it—you're showing your maturity and building trust.

THE DO'S AND DON'TS...
Waking Up Without Regret

DO: Program the numbers for two cab companies into your cell in case your Plan B falls asleep and misses your call. If you're too tired from your exciting night to drive yourself home, then don't. You can always call a cab and pick up your car in the morning.

DO: Use extra caution while driving. You may not drink at after-prom parties, but some other teens will. If you are behind the wheel, don't text, pick up any calls, or blast the music. It's just not worth it. It's also a smart idea to pack a comfy pair of shoes to drive in so you're not hitting the brakes in heels.

DON'T: Put your cup down at a party, even for just a minute. That leaves more than enough time for someone to slip something into your drink. Many drugs are colorless and odorless, so you won't even realize you're in a dangerous situation until the effects have already kicked in.

Have a DD on call

More than four thousand teens die every year in car accidents! Create a Plan B in case your night takes a shady turn: Make arrangements *before* prom night with a parent, older sibling, or trusted friend to pick you up—no questions asked—should you not feel comfortable and need a quick escape. Tell your backup ride that you'll text when you're home safely so they know when they're officially off-duty.

Brush off pressure to have sex

The first time your guy hints at having sex or doing anything else you're not comfortable with after prom, clear the air immediately so there's no awkwardness later. Be honest with him and simply say you're not ready to take your relationship there. A guy worth keeping will immediately understand; but if he tries to persuade you to change your mind, it's time for a new dude!

TO THINE OWN SELF BE TRUE

There's an electric excitement surrounding prom that makes it tempting to go along with whatever a big group of your friends and classmates are doing. You just want to have the most fun possible, right? That's normal, but—even though you see a glammed up version of your usual self in the reflection—stick with the decisions you would make any other day when it comes to safety. Not everyone is getting wasted, and booze isn't what makes or breaks the post-prom experience.

Notes

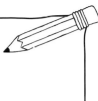

Notes

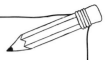

Notes

Part

POST-PROM

Was your prom night everything you imagined and more? Now that it's over, it's time to save your memories. Savor every important detail in Chapter 16— including those crazy times when you laughed so hard you cried! You'll also want to remember the little things, like where your prom was held, the theme of the night, what your date wore, and the songs you danced to, all night long, with all your best friends.

After weeks and weeks of waiting to wear your dream dress, now what should you do with it? Should you save it? Give it a brand-new look by cutting it and adding embellishments? Or should you pass along a bit of your prom night magic to another girl by donating your gown? Turn to page 138 for all that info and more—including how to turn your flowers into a decorative piece of art that you can keep forever.

And—although all the planning and partying is over—you can relive your prom night over and over again by printing your favorite photos and taping them to the scrapbooking pages in Chapter 16. There's also plenty of room for your family and friends to write special messages to you. These notes will make you smile for years to come and bring back all of the giddiness and excitement that filled this very special night.

15

WHAT TO DO WITH YOUR DRESS

You looked amazing in your prom dress—and you've got the photos to prove it!—but now that your special night is over, what's next for your gown? No matter what you decide to do with your dream dress, you'll want to have it dry cleaned first. But after that, you've got six great options:

DONATE IT!

If you bought a new dress, the best thing you can do with it is give it to another girl whose family may not have the extra money to buy a brand-new gown. You'll allow her to feel just as special and beautiful on prom night as you did, and that's major karma points! Visit DonateMyDress.org for information about how you can play fairy godmother for someone in your area. The site also has tips for organizing a prom dress drive if you and your friends want to make an even bigger impact!

TAKE IT TO THE TAILOR

A long gown isn't a closet staple that you'll wear again and again, but still, you can get more fashion miles out of your dress by making it a little less formal. Have your prom dress shortened to above your knee so it transforms into a fun party dress. You can also give it an entirely new vibe by adding or removing embellishments.

SAVE IT

If you want to keep your prom dress as-is as a reminder of your amazing night, you must take the right steps to preserve it. Fold and wrap your garment with acid-free tissue paper, then place it in an acid-free box. Keep it stored in a cool and dry environment (no damp garages!) to prevent discoloring.

SELL IT

Face it: Prom can cost a small fortune! To make some cash back, you can place your dress for sale on sites like eBay. You can also post your purse, heels, and jewelry for an even bigger payday. Excite buyers (and get more bids!) by taking plenty of well-lit photos of your items.

CREATE A COSTUME

Pull out your prom dress again next October and let your creativity run wild. Add a tiara and sash to become Miss Universe, or shorten your dress and buy wings to transform into a glamorous fairy on Halloween.

MAKE A KEEPSAKE

Frame more than just your prom photos. You can purchase a shadowbox at an arts-and-crafts store and display swatches of your dress's fabric, your fave picture from the night, a sparkly piece of jewelry—anything you want! It's a unique and personal way to forever remember your prom.

PRESS YOUR FLOWERS!

Your corsage looked almost as pretty as you, and luckily saving this part of your magical night is as easy as 1-2-3.

Step 1: Remove as many petals as you like a few days after prom when your flowers begin to slightly droop. Carefully place them in between two sheets of wax paper or newspaper pages without the petals touching.

Step 2: Stick those sheets or pages inside an old textbook or phonebook (be careful: It could stain the pages!), stack a few more heavy books on top, and let the pile sit for a week.

Step 3: Glue the pressed petals onto a piece of scrapbooking paper and frame. *Voila!*

16

LOOKING BACK

There are certain things about your prom that you'll always remember, things like the color of your dress, what you did with your friends after the dance, and the name of your date (I hope!). However, the little things—like the theme of your prom and what type of flowers your date gave you—are harder to recall over time. Because hey, you've a lot going on right now! So, while all the details are still fresh in your mind, lock up every memory right here.

Then, years from now, you can flip back to these pages and find a ready supply of hilarious, sweet, and surprising memories. It will all come flooding back.

Consider this your official prom time capsule.

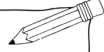

The Details

WHERE AND WHEN:

My prom was held on _____ from _____

p.m. until _____ p.m./a.m. at _____

_____ .

MY RIDE:

I drove a _____

to prom with _____ .

I had so much fun _____

_____

_____

_____ .

MY LOOK:

I wore a _____ dress that I bought

at _____ . What I loved most

about my entire look was _____

_____

MY DATE:

My date's name was _____ .

He wore a _____ .

The flowers he gave me were _____ .

The best part of bringing him as my date was _____

_____

_____

_____

_____

_____

_____ .

THE DANCE:

The theme of prom was _____ .

I danced to songs by _____

and _____ .

The last song was _____ .

Overall, my favorite moment from the dance was _____

_____

_____ .

DINNER:

_____ and I ate dinner at

_____ around _____ p.m.

I had _____ as my entrée

and it tasted _____ . For dessert I

had _____ . The craziest

thing happened at dinner, _____

_____

_____ .

THE AFTER-PARTY:

Once the dance ended, I _____ .

It was so great to _____ .

I finally ended up falling asleep at _____ .

Favorite Moments

Write down some of the best moments from your prom—the things you wish could happen over and over again.

Most Embarassing Moments

Use this space to savor the crazy, unexpected, hilarious, and embarrassing things that happened in the course of all your planning and promming.

Notes from friends and family

Just like you write in your friends' yearbooks, ask your friends, family, and your date—if you went with one—to write down a personal message that you can treasure forever.

Photos

Use these pages to tape photos from PRE-PROM parties.

Photos

Use these pages to tape photos from PROM.

Photos

Use these pages to tape photos from PROM.

Photos

Use these pages to tape photos from PROM AFTER.PARTY.